Baby animals in ocean habitats

Bobbie Kalman

🌱 Crabtree Publishing Company

www.crabtreebooks.com

Created by Bobbie Kalman

For my beautiful, sweet Alina, with much love from your Tante Bobbie

This book will help you teach your Oma Elfi how to speak English!

Author and Editor-in-Chief
Bobbie Kalman

Editors
Kathy Middleton
Crystal Sikkens

Design
Bobbie Kalman
Katherine Berti
Samantha Crabtree
(front cover)

Photo research
Bobbie Kalman

Print and production coordinator
Katherine Berti

Prepress technician
Katherine Berti

Illustrations
Katherine Berti: logo (coral), page 17
Tiffany Wybouw: page 8

Photographs
Dreamstime: pages 12, 24 (mammals)
iStockphoto: pages 18 (top), 19 (bottom left)
Photos.com: page 11 (right)
Other photographs by Shutterstock

Library and Archives Canada Cataloguing in Publication

Kalman, Bobbie, 1947-
    Baby animals in ocean habitats / Bobbie Kalman.

(The habitats of baby animals)
Includes index.
Issued also in electronic format.
ISBN 978-0-7787-7729-8 (bound).--ISBN 978-0-7787-7742-7 (pbk.)

    1. Marine animals--Infancy--Juvenile literature. 2. Marine ecology--Juvenile literature. I. Title. II. Series: Kalman, Bobbie, 1947- . Habitats of baby animals.

QL122.2.K343 2011   j591.3'909162   C2010-907523-4

Library of Congress Cataloging-in-Publication Data

Kalman, Bobbie.
    Baby animals in ocean habitats / Bobbie Kalman.
        p. cm. -- (The habitats of baby animals)
    Includes index.
    ISBN 978-0-7787-7742-7 (pbk. : alk. paper) -- ISBN 978-0-7787-7729-8 (reinforced library binding : alk. paper) -- ISBN 978-1-4271-9604-0 (electronic (pdf))
    1. Marine animals--Infancy--Juvenile literature. 2. Marine animals--Ecology--Juvenile literature. I. Title.
    QL122.2.K354 2011
    591.77--dc22
                                        2010047920

Crabtree Publishing Company

www.crabtreebooks.com   1-800-387-7650

Printed in China/022011/RG20101116

Published in Canada
Crabtree Publishing
616 Welland Ave.
St. Catharines, Ontario
L2M 5V6

Published in the United States
Crabtree Publishing
PMB 59051
350 Fifth Avenue, 59th Floor
New York, New York 10118

Published in the United Kingdom
Crabtree Publishing
Maritime House
Basin Road North, Hove
BN41 1WR

Published in Australia
Crabtree Publishing
386 Mt. Alexander Rd.
Ascot Vale (Melbourne)
VIC 3032

What is in this book?

What is a habitat?

A **habitat** is a place in nature. Plants and animals live in habitats. They are **living things**. Living things grow, change, and make new living things. Plants make new plants, and animals make babies. Habitats also have **non-living things**. Air, sunshine, rocks, soil, and water are non-living things. Living things need both non-living things and other living things. They find the things they need in their habitats.

What are oceans?

Oceans are huge areas of water. The water in oceans is **salt water**. Salt water contains a lot of salt. Some oceans are in parts of the world that have hot weather. These oceans have warm water. Some oceans are in parts of the world that have cold weather. These oceans have cold water and are covered with ice for part or all of the year. There are different kinds of habitats in oceans.

Five oceans on Earth

Earth is called the "blue planet" because it looks blue from space. It looks blue because water covers about three-quarters of Earth. The blue areas on this globe show where water is on Earth. The largest areas of water are oceans.

Arctic Ocean

Atlantic Ocean

Pacific Ocean

Southern Ocean

Five oceans

There are five oceans on Earth. From largest to smallest, they are the Pacific Ocean, Atlantic Ocean, Indian Ocean, Southern Ocean, and Arctic Ocean. The coldest oceans are the Southern Ocean and Arctic Ocean. The warmest ocean is the Indian Ocean. Some parts of the Atlantic Ocean and Pacific Ocean are in areas of the world that have four seasons.

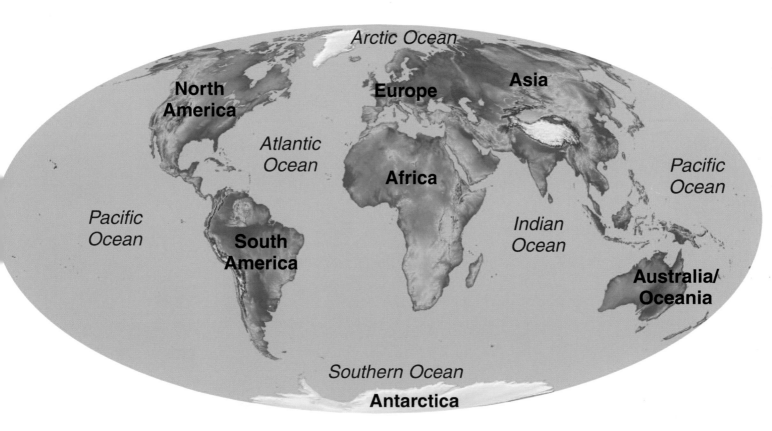

*Oceans flow around seven huge areas of land. These areas are called **continents**. The continents are Africa, Europe, Asia, South America, North America, Antarctica, and Australia/Oceania. Find the five oceans and seven continents on this map.*

Baby ocean animals

Some of the baby animals that live in oceans are dolphins, sea turtles, whales, polar bears, seals, penguins, moray eels, and many kinds of fish. These pages show a few ocean babies.

baby sea turtle

dolphin calf

narwhal calf with its mother

seal pup

baby clown fish

baby blue tang

baby moray eel

penguin chick

polar bear cub

9

Antarctic babies

The coldest ocean on Earth is the Southern Ocean. It flows around Antarctica. Not many kinds of animals can live in the Southern Ocean habitat, but penguins can. The water is so cold that the ocean is covered with ice for most of the year. All penguins have a thick layer of fat, called **blubber**, under their skin. Blubber keeps heat inside the bodies of penguins.

*Emperor penguins live in **colonies**, or large groups. These adult birds and their chicks are on the frozen ocean in Antarctica.*

Taking care of the chicks

Bird babies are called chicks. Chicks **hatch**. To hatch is to break out of an egg. Penguin mothers lay the eggs, but the fathers help keep the eggs warm. The fathers also keep the chicks warm after they hatch from their eggs.

Penguin parents feed their chicks by bringing up food for them from their stomachs.

Emperor penguin fathers have a flap over their feet that keeps an egg or chick warm.

Arctic babies

The Arctic Ocean is the smallest and shallowest of the five oceans. It touches the continents of Europe, Asia, and North America. The Arctic Ocean is freezing cold, just like the Southern Ocean. Penguins do not live there, but polar bears, some whales, and many kinds of seals do.

Polar bear cubs are well suited to their cold Arctic home. They have blubber as well as fur coats to keep them warm. Their fur is oily and waterproof, so their bodies do not get wet when they swim in the ocean.

Mammal mothers

Some animal mothers do not take care of their babies, but **mammal** mothers do. Mammal mothers make milk inside their bodies that they feed to their babies. Polar bears, seals, narwhals, and walruses are some mammals that live in the Arctic Ocean.

*Seal mothers **nurse** their babies, or feed them milk from their bodies.*

Narwhals are whales that live in the Arctic Ocean all year. They nurse their babies.

13

Warm-ocean babies

Warm oceans, such as the Indian Ocean and parts of the Pacific and Atlantic oceans, have colorful habitats called **coral reefs**. Coral reefs look like huge groups of plants, but they are not plants. Coral reefs are made up of animals called **coral polyps**. Many kinds of fish and other animals live in coral reef habitats.

coral

coral

coral polyps

This stingray and young squirrelfish live in a warm-ocean coral reef.

This whitetip reef shark pup is resting on sand at the bottom of a coral reef.
Two baby moray eels have found a place to hide among some corals.

15

Food in oceans

Animals need **energy**, or power, to breathe, move, grow, and stay alive. They get their energy from eating other living things. Plants make their own food. Ocean plants grow in sunny parts of oceans because they need sunlight to make food. Making food from sunlight is called **photosynthesis**.

*Green sea turtles are ocean **herbivores**. Herbivores eat plants. Most ocean animals are **carnivores**. Carnivores eat other animals.*

A coral reef food chain

Animals that live in ocean habitats find plenty of food to eat. Some ocean animals eat plants. Most ocean animals eat other animals. When an animal eats another animal that has eaten a plant, there is a **food chain**. The food chain on this page is made up of a sea plant, a blue tang, and a shark.

The shark eats the blue tang.

The blue tang eats plants.

Plants make their own food.

Sea turtle babies

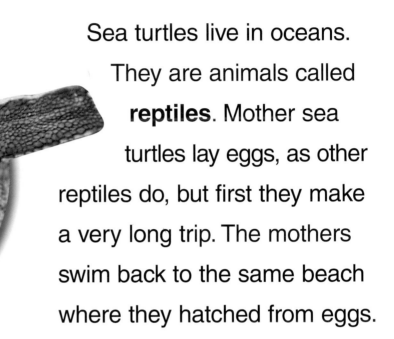

Sea turtles live in oceans. They are animals called **reptiles**. Mother sea turtles lay eggs, as other reptiles do, but first they make a very long trip. The mothers swim back to the same beach where they hatched from eggs.

This turtle is a leatherback sea turtle.

This sea turtle swam to the beach where she hatched. She is crawling along the sand to look for a safe spot. She will dig a hole and lay her eggs in it.

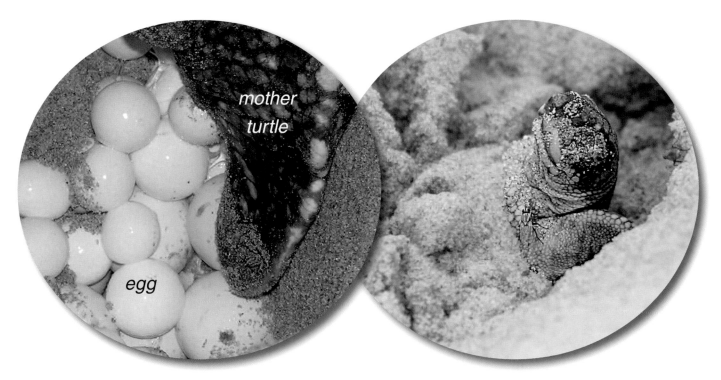

The mother leatherback is laying her eggs in the hole she dug in the sand.

After 7-10 weeks, the baby turtles start hatching and crawling out of the hole.

Most of the babies have now hatched. They crawl to the ocean and swim away.

Ocean travelers

Whales live in every ocean, but they do not always stay in one place. Some whales **migrate**, or travel long distances, to have their babies. Whales are mammals that give birth to live **calves**, or babies. Humpback whales live in cold oceans and travel to warm oceans to have their calves.

A baby whale has no blubber when it is born, so it would freeze to death in cold-ocean waters.

A calf is born

Female humpbacks give birth in warm water. A mother whale chooses a safe spot with shallow water so her baby can reach the surface of the water to breathe air when it is born. The mother lifts the calf above the water to take its first breath. The calf nurses about 40 times a day! Its mother's milk is very thick and rich. The calf grows quickly and puts on blubber. After several months, the mother whale swims home with her new calf.

At the end of winter, the whales start on their long journey back to the cold ocean. It can take up to three months for them to reach home.

Dolphin fun

Everyone loves dolphins! Dolphins are ocean mammals that make people happy. They always seem to be smiling, and they do things that entertain us. They leap high out of the water, spin, dance, and play games. They seem to have a lot of fun. How do you have fun?

Leap like a dolphin and ask your friends to leap with you!

Be curious like this baby dolphin and explore the world around you.

Smile like a dolphin, and you will feel happy. Your smile will make others feel happy, too.

Words to know and Index

babies
pages 4, 8–9, 10–11, 12–13, 14–15, 18–19, 20–21, 23

birds
pages 10–11

coral reefs
pages 14–15, 17

dolphins
pages 8, 22–23

food
pages 11, 13, 16–17

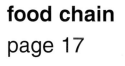

food chain
page 17

mammals
pages 13, 20, 22

mothers
pages 8, 11, 13, 18, 19, 21

nursing
pages 13, 21

Other index words
Antarctica pages 10–11
Arctic pages 12–13
carnivores page 16
habitats pages 4–5, 17
herbivores page 16
living things pages 4, 16
map of oceans page 7
non-living things page 4
oceans pages 5, 6–7, 8, 9, 10, 12, 13, 14, 15, 16, 17, 18, 19, 20, 21, 22
penguins pages 8, 10–11, 12
photosynthesis page 16
plants pages 4, 14, 16, 17
reptiles page 18
sea turtles pages 8, 16, 18–19
whales pages 8, 13, 20–21